Instant Citrix XenApp

A short guide for administrators to get the most out of the
Citrix XenApp 6.5 server farm

Andrew Mallett

BIRMINGHAM - MUMBAI

Instant Citrix XenApp

First published: July 2013

Production Reference: 1190713

Published by Packt Publishing Ltd.

Livery Place
35 Livery Street
Birmingham B3 2PB, UK.

ISBN 978-1-78217-026-6

www.packtpub.com

Credits

Author

Andrew Mallett

Reviewer

John Cumpsty

Acquisition Editor

Andrew Duckworth

Akram Hussain

Commissioning Editor

Priyanka Shah

Technical Editors

Jalasha D'costa

Rikita Poojari

Project Coordinator

Michelle Quadros

Proofreader

Lucy Rowland

Production Coordinator

Melwyn D'sa

Cover Work

Melwyn D'sa

Cover Image

Disha Haria

About the Author

Andrew Mallett has worked in the field of IT for more years than he cares to mention, well since 1986, and he has been working with Citrix technologies since Metaframe 1.8 in 1999. Not only does he possess Citrix skills and the relevant certification, he is able to teach Linux, Citrix, Novell, and Microsoft official courses, and supports many of these products.

Andrew currently works as a freelance instructor and author in the UK, and teaching Citrix and Linux throughout Europe. You can follow his exploits on Twitter (@theurbanpenguin) and review his video tutorials on his website located at http://www.theurbanpenguin.com. If you prefer Facebook, then you have http://www.facebook.com/Theurbanpenguin.

Andrew has previously authored the *Citrix Access Gateway VPX 5.04 Essentials, Packt Publishing* and has worked as a technical reviewer for the book *Instant Citrix Security How-to, Packt Publishing*.

About the Reviewer

John Cumpsty has worked in the IT industry since 1984, having begun with Digital Equipment Corporation in its DecDirect operation as a Product Manager for its Networking Products line. This experience subsequently led to working in a variety of Product Marketing and Sales roles for a number of smaller U.S. and UK manufacturers who wished to penetrate UK and other European IT markets. A number of these products were complementary to the solutions being brought to market by Citrix in the mid 90s, and so having been "hooked on Citrix", there was a certain logic in John becoming a Citrix Certified Instructor, which has been the case since November 1999.

Most of his CCI experience, knowledge, and skills have come through employment with UK CALCs, but for the last 4 years he has provided training on a freelance basis in conjunction with UK, other European, and Middle East Citrix channels.

John provides Citrix training through his own company, Fulcrum Learning Services Limited, and can be reached by e-mail at john.cumpsty@fulcrumls.co.uk.

www.packtpub.com

Support files, eBooks, discount offers and more

You might want to visit www.packtpub.com for support files and downloads related to your book.

Did you know that Packt offers eBook versions of every book published, with PDF and ePub files available? You can upgrade to the eBook version at www.packtpub.com and as a print book customer, you are entitled to a discount on the eBook copy. Get in touch with us at service@packtpub.com for more details.

At www.packtpub.com, you can also read a collection of free technical articles, sign up for a range of free newsletters and receive exclusive discounts and offers on Packt books and eBooks.

packtlib.packtpub.com

Do you need instant solutions to your IT questions? PacktLib is Packt's online digital book library. Here you can access, read and search across Packt's entire library of books.

Why Subscribe?

- ✦ Fully searchable across every book published by Packt
- ✦ Copy and paste, print and bookmark content
- ✦ On demand and accessible via web browser

Free Access for Packt account holders

If you have an account with Packt at www.packtpub.com, you can use this to access PacktLib today and view nine entirely free books. Simply use your login credentials for immediate access.

Table of Contents

Instant Citrix XenApp   **1**

So, what is Citrix XenApp?   **3**

Installation   **5**
- Step 1 – servers that XenApp requires   5
- Step 2 – installing the licensing server   5
- Step 3 – installing XenApp Server and SQL Express   6
- Step 4 – installing the Web Interface server   9
- And that's it   10

Quick start – publishing applications   **11**
- Step 1 – connecting with AppCenter   11
- Step 2 – publishing an application using AppCenter   11
- Step 3 – publishing applications using PowerShell   13
- Step 4 – publishing server desktops   13
- Step 5 – publishing content   14
- Step 6 – prelaunching applications   14
- Step 7 – accessing published applications   15

Top 14 features you need to know about   **16**
- Delegating administration   16
- Managing worker groups   17
- Utilizing Group Policies   18
- Assigning ICA session timeouts   19
- Controlling access to ICA virtual channels   21
- Session lingering   21
- Demystifying printing within XenApp   22
- Enabling IMA encryption   25
- Load management   26
- Controlling access to servers   28
- Restricting the domains that can log on to the Web Interface   29

Customizing the Web Interface   30
Providing secure remote access to XenApp   32
Monitoring XenApp   33
People and places you should get to know   **35**
Official sites   35
Articles and tutorials   35
Blogs   35
Twitter   35

Instant Citrix XenApp

Welcome to *Instant Citrix XenApp*. This book has been especially created to provide you with all the information you will need to get started with XenApp 6.5. You will learn the basics of Citrix XenApp and build your first server farm. With this in place, we will be publishing applications and resources to our users' community and managing their connectivity. Particular attention is paid to achieving tasks both from the GUI and the command line using Microsoft PowerShell wherever applicable, allowing you to choose how you would like to manage your farm.

This document contains the following sections:

So, what is XenApp? helps you find out what XenApp actually is, and what it provides, above and beyond Microsoft Remote Desktop Services (RDS).

Installation teaches you how to install the XenApp Server and other resources that are required for a XenApp server farm.

Quick start – publishing applications will show you how to perform one of the core tasks of XenApp: making applications available to remote users. We will do this by using the consoles and the command line using PowerShell.

Top 14 features you need to know about will teach you how to manage the most common tasks in XenApp including Group Policy settings, load evaluators, and secure access.

People and places you should get to know provides you with many useful links to the project page and forums, as well as a number of helpful articles, tutorials, blogs, and the Twitter feeds of those in the XenApp know, as every high profile project is centered on a group of evangelists as well as the organization.

So, what is Citrix XenApp?

XenApp server 6.5 is the current remote desktop server solution from Citrix, a Florida-based company. It is reliant on **Remote Desktop Service** (**RDS**) and Microsoft Windows Server 2008 R2; however, XenApp expands upon the functionality purely offered by Microsoft.

By remote desktop server, we mean that users can connect remotely to the desktop or published applications on that server. More often than not, users connect to published applications and not the server desktop (Citrix XenDesktop providing the specialist connectivity to desktops). Once connected to the published application or server desktop, the applications run using the server's resources such as memory and CPU, and regardless of the connectivity that the user has, however remote, the application will run as if it were local to the user. One major advantage that Citrix provides against the competition is that the user's local device can be virtually any computing device from a Windows PC to Apple Computers (Mac), Linux desktops, smart phones, and also tablet PCs that include the Chromebook and Blackberry PlayBook as well as the more obvious iPads and Android devices.

Now that we know the device can connect remotely, we have to make sure that it has the Citrix client, or what is known as the **Receiver** installed (the Receiver can be downloaded from Citrix (http://www.citrix.com/downloads/citrix-receiver.html), or from central application repositories such as Apple's AppStore and Google Play). Once installed, the Receiver can make a connection to the XenApp server farm, and a list of available resources displayed back to the user. The connection will use the proprietary Citrix protocol, **Independent Computing Architecture** (**ICA**). This highlights more advantages that XenApp offers:

✦ Virtual channels that can be independently controlled for desktop features such as clipboard, printing, sound, and drive mapping

✦ Local Flash playback that can play Adobe Flash movies on a local device rather than a server

✦ Windows media redirection, as with Flash, can be compressed and can send movie and sound files to the client to play locally-freeing resources on the server (if the client has the correct local software)

✦ Integration with Microsoft Lync server for video conferencing

All in all, the architecture used for client-to-server communications can greatly reduce the bandwidth required on a recent project where the requirement is for local PCs to scan customer's correspondence, using remote application servers. We established baselines that each client required, on an average of 250 Kbps using Microsoft RDS compared to 100 Kbps when using Citrix XenApp 6.5.

The scanner would be attached to the client's device; however, the scanning software will run within XenApp. The input from the scanner is transferred, in this case via the TWAIN virtual channel of the ICA connection, from the client to the server.

Besides the Citrix XenApp servers that will host the users' sessions, we will need other server resources such as:

- ✦ A database server to host the farm database

- ✦ A license server to issue concurrent user licenses

- ✦ A Web Interface server to present resources to the user that are available on the XenApp Server

Ideally, these all would be on separate servers, but a single server can potentially provide all server resources, including XenApp. This would not be recommended but is acceptable for a proof of concept system, where the need to demonstrate XenApp is required.

Management is maintained through the graphical tool Citrix AppCenter, for those needing a more scriptable style of management. PowerShell modules are provided to allow easy command-line capabilities. In the following screenshot Citrix AppCenter is shown:

XenApp gives you and your users the ability to run applications remotely, as if they were in the office, regardless of the devices they connect from. This enables greater productivity and flexibility in working arrangements. Within your main office, user desktops can be replaced with thin devices that require little or no maintenance, and can additionally reduce power consumption from an average of 400 watts to 5 watts per device.

Installation

In four easy steps, you can install and configure a XenApp 6.5 server farm, and be ready to publish hosted applications.

Step 1 – servers that XenApp requires

XenApp requires additional services to be installed. All of these can be on a single server for a proof of concept system, but in production environments, the services are often separated out. These are as follows:

+ A licensing server: The licensing server software can be installed onto Windows 2003 through 2008 R2, and additionally Windows 7. For XenApp, the licensing server provides concurrent users' licenses. The license server software ships on the XenApp installation DVD.

+ Microsoft SQL 2005/2008 or Oracle 11*g* database server: The farm database needs to be installed and managed on a database server. This can include SQL Express, if you do not currently have licenses for the full database server.

+ A Web Interface server: The Citrix Receiver will make its connection initially to the Web Interface server, which is a required component of the XenApp farm.

All of the previous components are included in the XenApp 6.5 installation DVD.

Step 2 – installing the licensing server

During the configuration of XenApp, you are prompted for the license server, and it is considered best practice to install it ahead of time. The license server can be shared with other Citrix products such as XenDesktop and XenServer; the minimum version number required for XenApp 6.5 is Version 11.9, which ships with the installation DVD. The license server will require the following TCP ports to be opened if currently blocked by firewalls:

+ **8082**: Web Console

+ **7279**: This is known as the Vendor Daemon Port; end user licenses are checked in and checked out on this port

+ **27000**: The XenApp servers will check the availability of the license server on this port

When purchased, licenses can be downloaded from the MyCitrix website at http://www.citrix.com/mycitrix. Your own MyCitrix ID can be linked to your company's licenses for management.

Not only will you need concurrent user licenses for XenApp, but you will also require valid Remote Desktop Services licenses for each XenApp server that will host user sessions. Citrix licenses are concurrent user and RDS licenses are per user or per device.

Installing the licenses is managed through a web console to the license server on port 8082. This can be seen in the following screenshot:

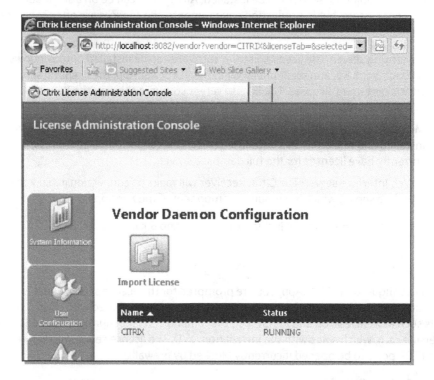

Step 3 – installing XenApp Server and SQL Express

The XenApp 6.5 Server has to be installed on Microsoft Windows Server 2008 R2. The .NET Framework 3.51 is also required as is the Remote Desktop Servers role. Installing the XenApp Server from the integrated installer will add these roles and features if needed.

XenApp can be installed on physical or virtual machines. XenApp can run with as low an amount of resources as the operating system will allow, for example, 1 GB RAM; however, we would recommend scaling your server's memory and CPU to support the applications that you will be hosting on the server.

If you do not have an existing SQL Server infrastructure, it is possible to install SQL Express when creating the farm database. This will be achieved as the first XenApp Server is added to the farm. For the purposes of this book, we will use this method, although for a database with high availability and speed of access, a full standalone version of SQL is recommended. Using the integrated installer at the root of the XenApp 6.5 installation DVD, `autorun.exe`, we can start the installation, and choose to install XenApp Server from the first screen as shown in the following screenshot:

Continuing through the installation screens, we choose to add server roles. Choose the edition of XenApp that we have licensed (Platinum, Enterprise, or Advanced), read and accept the license agreement, and we arrive at the XenApp server role screen, as shown in the following screenshot:

Choose XenApp roles

Choose the roles you want to add to this server below.   What roles should I include in my farm?

⊿ **Common Roles**
- ☐ **License Server** ⓘ
- ☐ **XenApp** ⓘ
- ☐ **Receiver Storefront** ⓘ
- ☐ Merchandising Server ⓘ
  (This is a virtual appliance and requires a virtual machine.)

⊿ **Other Roles**
- ☐ **Single Sign-on Service** ⓘ
- ☐ **Secure Gateway** ⓘ
- ☐ **Power and Capacity Management Administration** ⓘ
- ☐ **EdgeSight Server** ⓘ
- ☐ **Provisioning Services** ⓘ
- ☐ **SmartAuditor Server** ⓘ
- ☐ **Web Interface** ⓘ

From here, we will choose to install XenApp and accept the default subroles. The server will require a reboot once the installation is complete. Upon reboot, we are taken into the server configuration tool, where we first specify the licensing server, and create a XenApp server farm. In specifying the database server, we choose the option to create the database: do not misinterpret this. It will both install SQL Express and create the database, so always read the small print as shown in the following screenshot:

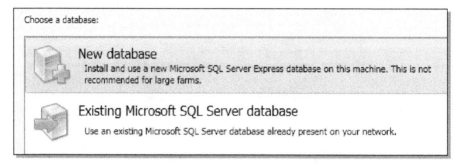

One major feature of XenApp 6.5 is that it allows for more control of the election of the **Zone Data Collector** (**ZDC**). The farm database holds the static information about the farm; this includes servers, administrators, and applications. Dynamic information is collated in the memory of the ZDC. A ZDC is elected for each zone and the ZDC maintains the list of users' sessions and XenApp server load. Prior to XenApp 6.5, every XenApp server would, by default, participate in the election process. To streamline the election process in 6.5, only XenApp servers with the session controller role mode can participate in the election. The first server in the farm has to have both the session controller and the session host mode, but subsequent servers could have just the session host role. As we have just one server in our farm, it must have both the modes, as can be seen from the following screenshot:

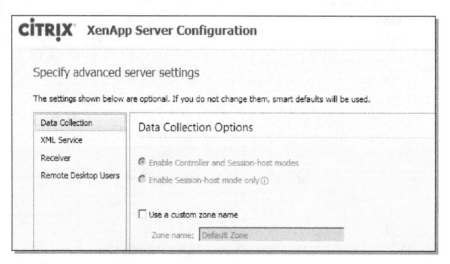

TCP ports that need to be open for XenApp include the following:

+ **80**: The Citrix XML Service

+ **1494**: ICA sessions

+ **2512**: This represents the IMA XenApp server-to-server communication

+ **2513**: This represents the AppCenter and PowerShell connections

+ **2598**: This represents the HDX session reliability allowing interruptions of the ICA session without re-authenticating

+ **3389**: This can be used for Remote Desktop Sessions using the Microsoft protocol but is less feature-rich than the ICA protocol

Step 4 – installing the Web Interface server

The Web Interface server is a required component of both XenApp and XenDesktop. With XenApp, no matter how the clients make their connection (either via the browser or direct from the Citrix Receiver), the initial connection request will go through the Web Interface. The Web Interface will authenticate users and communicate with the session controllers (known as the **XML Brokers**) to identify for users the most suitable XenApp server to host the ICA session.

The following illustration shows that connections made either through the web browser or the dedicated Citrix Receiver require the Web Interface server. The browser using the Web Site and Receiver requires the Services Site:

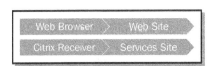

The Web Interface Version 5.4 can be installed on Windows Server 2003 R2 SP2 and higher, and this version ships with the XenApp installation DVD. The Web Interface server, like the license server, can be shared across farms and products.

From the management console, Citrix Web Interface Management (which is installed along with the server) we need to add our XenApp server farm to the existing Web Interface sites, or alternatively, create sites that can be used for clients. The two sites that can be created are:

+ **Web Site**: To accept client connections from supported web browsers
+ **Services Site**: To accept client connections directly from the Citrix Receiver

Using an existing Web Site, we right-click on the Web Site and choose **Server Farms** from the context menu. In the subsequent dialog, we add the farm name and session controller addresses of servers in the farm. The right-click menu is shown in the following screenshot:

 Web Interface sites can be managed graphically via the management console we have just seen, or using the `webinterface.conf` configuration file. Although the GUI is the tool of choice for many administrators, the configuration file can be used to duplicate settings across more than one Web Interface servers.

And that's it

By this point you should have a working XenApp 6.5 farm, and we are now ready to start publishing applications.

Quick start – publishing applications

XenApp 6.5 can of course provide remote access to applications; however, besides this, XenApp can publish server desktops and resources such as web pages and documents. In this section, we will cover publishing these resources using both AppCenter and PowerShell.

Step 1 – connecting with AppCenter

AppCenter is installed along with the XenApp server; however, if required, it can be installed onto a client machine.

✦ Often AppCenter is run remotely by administrators who connect to the XenApp server's desktop. Use the following path to run AppCenter:

Start | Administrative Tools | Citrix | Management Consoles | Citix AppCenter

✦ The first time the console is run, it is necessary to discover the farm. We can do this by selecting to add the local computer (this is usual if we are running AppCenter on the XenApp Server). Ensure that we only discover XenApp, and not **Single Sign-on** (**SSO**) servers.

✦ If connecting remotely from AppCenter to XenApp, instead of discovering the local computer, we would add the IP address of any XenApp Server in the farm and ensure we have connectivity on TCP port 2513.

Step 2 – publishing an application using AppCenter

When users connect to the Web Interface server, they are presented with a list of applications that they may access. To create published applications with AppCenter:

✦ If you want an application to appear in the list, it must be "published". Navigating to the **Application** node of AppCenter, we can use the right-click menu and select the option **Publish Application**. As we run through the wizard, for our example, we will choose to publish notepad.exe.

✦ Set the application name.

✦ Set the application type by selecting **Application | Accessed from a Server | Installed application**. Applications can be installed or streamed to servers. We can see from the following screenshot the application type page from the wizard:

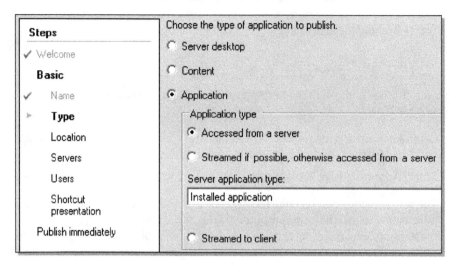

✦ As the wizard continues, we choose the remaining options as follows:

1. Set the executable's name and location.

2. Set the servers that will host the application. This could be a list of server names from the farm, or the assignment could be to a group of servers known as a **worker group**.

3. Assign user access to the application by selecting, most usually, domain groups on the users page of the wizard.

4. Finally, we can choose to add the application to folders either on the web page or start menu depending on the type of access.

The properties that we set here are the basic properties, and once set, the application can be published immediately.

Step 3 – publishing applications using PowerShell

Besides using the GUI AppCenter, it is also possible to add and configure published applications with PowerShell. The following steps will guide you to do the same:

1. The PowerShell modules are installed along with the XenApp Server, but as with AppCenter, it can be added to client machines if required.

2. If it is required to install the snap-ins independently to XenApp, we would navigate the installation DVD to the `<INSTALLDVD>:\Administration\Delivery Services Console\setup` folder. From the `Citrix.XenApp.Commands.Client.Install_x86` folder we can install the snap-ins for a 32-bit platform and from `Citrix.XenApp.Commands.Client.Install_x64` for the 64-bit architecture.

3. Once we have a PowerShell prompt open, we will need to load the required snap-in:

    ```
    Add-PSSnapin Citrix.XenApp.Commands
    ```

4. With the snap-in loaded, we create the new application:

    ```
    New-XAApplication -BrowserName Notepad -ApplicationType
    ServerInstalled -DisplayName Notepad -CommandLineExecutable
    "notepad.exe" -ServerNames XA1
    ```

5. The application can be associated with users with the following PowerShell command:

    ```
    Add-XAApplicationAccount Notepad "Example\Domain Users"
    ```

6. Finally, the application will need to be enabled with this last line of code:

    ```
    Set-XAApplication Notepad -Enabled $true
    ```

Step 4 – publishing server desktops

If required, users can access a server desktop. For this, the application type would be set to `Server Desktop`.

By default, only administrators are allowed access to published desktops in XenApp. For other users, this can be enabled using Citrix Group Policies as shown in the following screenshot from a Citrix User Policy (Group Policies are covered in more detail later):

Desktop launches
ICA   Add

Step 5 – publishing content

The published content can be web URL or files on network shares accessible by the client from the XenApp Server. The content may be in the form of PDF documentation or in the form of access to intranet sites that the users will need access to. We can see from the following screenshot that we can provide shortcuts to web resources such as the licensing server web console:

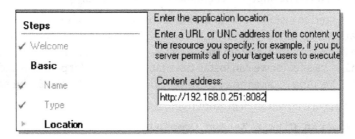

Step 6 – prelaunching applications

You will soon note that launching an application for the first time takes a little time as the client device has to establish a session on the server. This involves running login scripts, evaluating policies, and loading the user's profile. Once the session is established, other applications launch more quickly on the same server as they share the existing session.

The session exists until the user logs out from all applications. When accessing applications using the Web Interface Services Site with the Citrix Receiver, it is possible to configure session prelaunch. This is achieved by creating a prelaunch application from one of our published applications. When a user logs onto the receiver, a session is then created for him/her immediately or at a scheduled time. This gives faster access to the applications as the session pre-exists.

[A user license is used as soon as the user logs on onto the Receiver, not just when they launch apps.]

To create a prelaunch application, right-click on an existing application and from the context menu select **Other Tasks | Create pre-launch application,** as shown in the following screenshot:

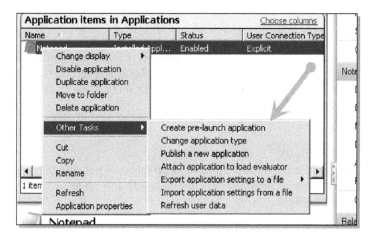

Step 7 – accessing published applications

We are now ready to test the connection and we will connect to the Web Interface Web Site.

 The Web Interface Services Site is for direct connections from the
Citrix Receiver; the Web Interface Web Site is used by the web browser
and online plugins.

The default Web Site will be `http://<yourwebinterfaceserver>/Citrix/XenApp`. You
will be prompted for your username and password, and possibly your domain name. Once
authenticated, you can see a list of your applications associated with your login, content, and
desktops. From the following screenshot, we can see the published application, that is, Notepad:

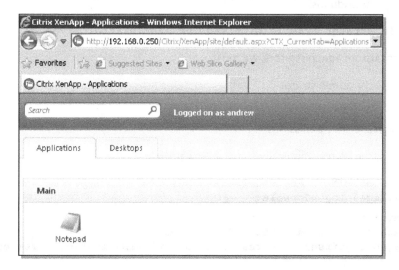

Top 14 features you need to know about

As you start to manage your XenApp server farm, you will realize that some configuration settings will work well with the defaults, while others will not. The setting that won't work well will have to be tuned for your specific environment. In this section, we investigate some of the main administrative areas of Citrix XenApp 6.5.

Delegating administration

The administrative user that creates the initial XenApp farm will become the only farm administrator. Almost certainly, your first task will be to add at least an additional administrative group as farm administrators.

Administrators can have three levels of privileges:

+ Full administrators
+ View-only administrators
+ Custom administrators

Both full and view-only administration applies to the complete farm, whereas custom administration applies only to the assigned folders. Permissions can only be assigned at the folder level in XenApp, and not to an individual element. For example, we can assign administrative permissions to the application folder but not to individual applications.

New administrators are added using the **Administrators** node of AppCenter, or by using PowerShell. The following PowerShell code can be run once the Citrix PSSnapin, `Citrix.XenApp.Commands`, is loaded and will create a full XenApp administrator based on the domain group CitrixAdmins:

```
New-XAAdministrator Example\CitrixAdmins -AdministratorType Full
```

When adding custom administrators, we must:

+ Create the administrator
+ Set the context where they should have rights
+ Assign specific permissions

This, as before, can be set graphically, or using PowerShell:

```
New-XAAdministrator Example\HelpDesk -AdministratorType Custom
-FarmPrivileges LogonConsole

Set-XAAdministratorFolder Example\HelpDesk
-FolderPath Applications -FolderPrivileges
sendmessages,logoffsessions,resetsessions,viewapplications,viewsessions
```

Managing worker groups

In a XenApp 6.5 server farm, worker groups are used to group XenApp servers together. These groups can be used when publishing applications, assigning Group Policies, and with load-balancing policies allowing for controlled failover to remote data centers.

Populating worker groups can be achieved using the following:

+ Active Directory **organizational units (OUs)**
+ Active Directory groups
+ Individual farm servers

This can be seen from the wizard used to create worker groups in the following screenshot:

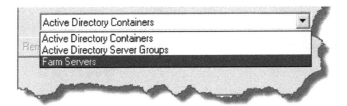

If you need to script the creation of worker groups, or if you prefer to work from the command line, then the same can be achieved using PowerShell.

In the example code, we first test to see if the required snap-in is loaded, and if it is not, then we load the snap-in. The worker group is created with the New-XAWorkerGroup cmdlet and will initially include the XenApp servers XA1 and XA2. We then add a new server to the group, and finally we see how we can delete the group.

```
if ( (Get-PSSnapin -Name Citrix.XenApp.Commands -ErrorAction
SilentlyContinue) -eq $null )
  {
    Add-PsSnapin Citrix.XenApp.Commands
  }
New-XAWorkerGroup -WorkerGroupName "All Servers" -ServerNames XA1,XA2
```

To add additional servers to the worker group later, we can use Set-XAWorkergroup:

Set-XAWorkerGroup "All Servers" -ServerNames XA1,XA2,XA3

The issue you may have identified with adding to the member list of the worker group is that we have to re-enter the existing names; however, Citrix quite cleverly overcomes this with the following two cmdlets:

+ Add-XAWorkerGroupServer
+ Remove-XAWorkerGroupServer

The names are not that descriptive, as the cmdlets can respectively add or remove servers, server groups or OUs to/from worker groups. Firstly, let us look at creating a worker group based on Active Directory server groups. This is an effective way of managing worker groups if your Citrix administration teams have rights to the **Active Directory** (**AD**), as the group management then exists solely in the AD.

```
New XA-WorkerGroup BRM -ServerGroups Example\BRMServers
```

The worker group is now created and contains the Active Directory group BRMServers. To append additional servers, groups, or OUs to this worker group, we can simply use:

```
Add-XAWorkerGroupServer BRM -Servergroups Example\MCRServers
```

The worker group will now contain both the server groups. Incidentally, we can mix and match the membership. For instance, we can continue to append to the group, this time adding in a single farm server:

```
Add-XAWorkerGroupServer BRM -ServerNames XA1
```

The group now contains the two Active Directory groups, and the single farm server within its membership. In a similar fashion, we can remove items from the membership list:

```
Remove-XAWorkerGroupServer BRM -ServerNames XA1
```

If it is required to delete a worker group completely, then with PowerShell we could issue the following command:

```
Remove-XAWorkerGroup "All Servers"
```

Utilizing Group Policies

Most of your administration needs in Citrix will turn out to be resolvable using Group Policies. Using XenDesktop 5 or XenApp 6, and later Citrix, go beyond simple templates and utilize Group Policy Management Extensions. During the installation of XenApp 6.5, these extensions are installed onto the XenApp servers along with AppCenter and the PowerShell modules, but can be installed independently onto other Windows systems. They can be used either with AppCenter or with the Microsoft Group Policy Management MMC.

To install the Citrix Group Policy Extensions independently from XenApp, such as when you wish to install the extensions onto your own desktop, navigate through the XenApp installation DVD to the <INSTALLDVD>:\Administration\Delivery Services Console\setup folder. From here, we will install the appropriate Citrix Group Policy Management MSI, either the 32-bit or 64-bit version.

Group Policies can be set in AppCenter, and can become local **Independent Management Architecture** (**IMA**) Group Policies. If they are set using Group Policy Management, they are stored in the Active Directory. Local IMA policies are limited to the scope of the farm, whereas Active Directory policies can be effective across farms, and XenApp and XenDesktop can share the same policies.

Computer policies can be filtered on the worker group and applied to XenApp servers. User policies are more flexible and can be filtered on criteria, which include the client IP address, user group, device name, and so on. For each policy, there is always one unfiltered policy that can affect all computers or users unless later overwritten with a specific filtered policy.

If you're using PowerShell to manage Group Policies, a PowerShell drive is automatically assigned to the local IMA Group Policy. If you need to manage Active Directory policies from PowerShell, you will first need to add a PowerShell drive pointing to the Active Directory policy. The required PowerShell snap-in is `Citrix.Common.GroupPolicy`. Once the PowerShell snap-in is loaded, we can use `Get-PSDrive` to display the drive assigned to the IMA Group Policy. This is shown in the following screenshot (you will notice the very last line as the PSDrive `LocalFarmGpo`):

```
PS C:\Users\administrator.EXAMPLE> Get-PSDrive

Name          Used (GB)      Free (GB)  Provider      Root
----          ---------      ---------  --------      ----
Alias                                   Alias
C               10.28          13.62    FileSystem    C:\
cert                                    Certificate   \
D                4.40                   FileSystem    D:\
Env                                     Environment
Function                                Function
HKCU                                    Registry      HKEY_CURRENT_USER
HKLM                                    Registry      HKEY_LOCAL_MACHINE
LocalFa...                              CitrixGrou... LocalFarmGpo:\
```

If you need to connect to an Active Directory-based policy, you will need to create a drive letter pointing to the Group Policy. This can be achieved with code similar to the following example:

```
New-PSDrive XA -root \ -PSProvider CitrixGroupPolicy -Domain "XenApp
Policy"
```

The drive letter created will be `XA:`, in this case, and the target in the Active Directory is a policy named `XenApp Policy`.

Assigning ICA session timeouts

If a user disconnects from his/her ICA session, the session remains in effect and will continue to use resources on the server and a license. Some users are not aware of the difference between disconnecting and logging out. It may be appropriate to add in a disconnection timeout, allowing users to disconnect, but, if they do not reconnect within a certain time interval, the session is then terminated. Policies can be set using the **Policies** node of AppCenter or using the Group Policy Management tool from Microsoft. User policies are refreshed on the interval, normally 90 minutes or during the logon process. In the following example, we demonstrate, using PowerShell, setting the local IMA Group Policy with a 60-minute disconnect interval.

```
Set-ItemProperty LocalFarmGPO:\User\Unfiltered\Settings\ICA\
SessionLimits\SessionDisconnectTimer -Name State -Value Enabled

Set-ItemProperty LocalFarmGPO:\User\Unfiltered\Settings\ICA\
SessionLimits\SessionDisconnectTimerInterval -Name Value -Value 60
```

`Set-ItemProperty LocalFarmGPO:` is written on a single line. So, we have two lines of code here, each beginning with `Set-ItemProperty`. The line happens to wrap for the purpose of the book.

Here, the PowerShell code enables the disconnection timeout and sets the timer to 60 minutes. This can be shown through AppCenter in the following screenshot:

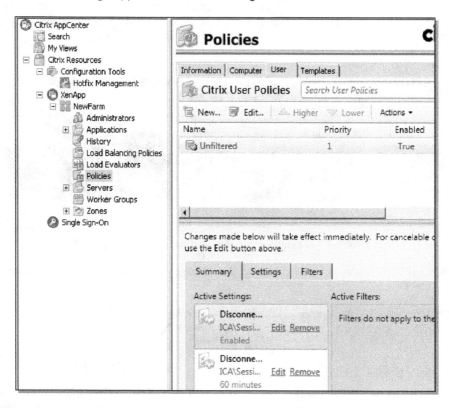

Controlling access to ICA virtual channels

Remote access to the XenApp server is great, but we have to keep in mind the security of the corporate data. The default settings will allow for the mapping of the client clipboard and local drive mappings. This would allow remote users to store data on the client machines, so it may be necessary to disallow this in the unfiltered policy, allowing it for a specific policy that applies to your internal IP address range:

```
Set-ItemProperty LocalFarmGPO:\User\Unfiltered\Settings\ICA\
FileRedirection\ClientDriveRedirection -Name State -Value Prohibited
```

```
Set-ItemProperty LocalFarmGPO:\User\Unfiltered\Settings\ICA\
ClipboardRedirection -Name State -Value Prohibited
```

[When using PowerShell, you can use the *Tab* key to complete the item names. So, this becomes practically a lot easier than it may look at first.]

Session lingering

We saw earlier, as we studied the gentle art of publishing applications, that it was possible to create prelaunch applications that can establish a session ahead of the user launching the specific application. Session prelaunch is available for users who log in to the Citrix Receiver to the Services Site, rather than using the web browser. Even with prelaunch, if a user logs out, they will find that the next application startup will be extended. This is because the session needs to be re-established. Users may often close one application before starting another, and this has the effect of logging them out of their session. To overcome this, we may allow a session to "linger" after termination. The word linger is often associated with unpleasant characters, with nothing good in mind. With Citrix, lingering is good and this is normally only for a short time –in the following example we use 5 minutes. This has the positive effect of keeping the user's session alive as one application closes and another starts within the interval. The linger timeout is available to be used no matter how the user connects, making the setting effective for browser and Receiver connections, and is not reliant upon session prelaunch:

```
Set-ItemProperty LocalFarmGPO:\User\Unfiltered\Settings\ICA\
SessionLimits\LingerTerminateTimerInterval -Name Value -Value 5
```

Demystifying printing within XenApp

The default printing settings in XenApp allow for all the client printers to be connected to the session automatically and more disconcertingly, to load the native print drivers on the servers. While the printers exist only for the length of the user's session, the drivers become a permanent feature of the XenApp server once loaded. Even though we may want to connect client printers for some users, there are a few policies that we should implement in order to optimize the printing environment. From the following screenshot, we can see some user policies that we should consider for taming printing within XenApp:

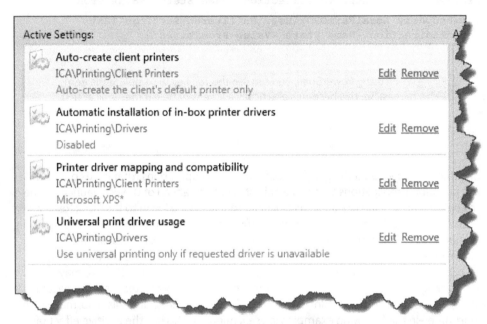

Firstly, we see that the policy only autocreates the client's default printer. For home machines, it is possible that many printers will exist, but only one is ever used, the default printer. Mapping only the default printer makes great sense and the knock-on effect across hundreds of users will be immense in taming the printing environment within XenApp.

```
Set-ItemProperty LocalFarmGPO:\User\Unfiltered\Settings\ICA\
Printing\ClientPrinters\ClientPrinterAutoCreation -Name Value -Value
DefaultPrinterOnly
```

Directly following this, we disable loading of drivers on the XenApp servers. If the print driver is not loaded on the server already (perhaps having been authorized by a Citrix administrator), the native print driver will not load on the XenApp server:

```
Set-ItemProperty LocalFarmGPO:\User\Unfiltered\Settings\ICA\Printing\
Drivers\InBoxDriverAutoInstallation -Name State -Value Disabled
```

The next setting disables the connection of client print drivers that begin with `Microsoft XPS*`. This prevents mapping of the Microsoft XPS Document Writer which, in many instances, no one uses and will often exist on the XenApp server, which makes a client version superfluous.

```
Set-ItemProperty LocalFarmGPO:\User\Unfiltered\Settings\ICA\Printing\
ClientPrinters\PrinterDriverMappings -Name Values -Value @("Microsoft
XPS*,Deny")
```

The final setting shown in the previous screenshot also represents the default setting for the Universal print driver. It will automatically be used if the native driver is not available. So, for those users where their printer driver is not already loaded on the XenApp server, they will use the Universal driver from Citrix.

```
Set-ItemProperty LocalFarmGPO:\User\Unfiltered\Settings\ICA\Printing\
Drivers\UniversalPrintDriverUsage -Name Value -Value FallBackToUPD
```

Configuring Group Policies can be done graphically or using PowerShell. We have seen the configuration made with PowerShell here, and of course these settings could all be made from executing a PowerShell script. If you prefer to work graphically, the following screenshot highlights the Group Policy settings we have implemented:

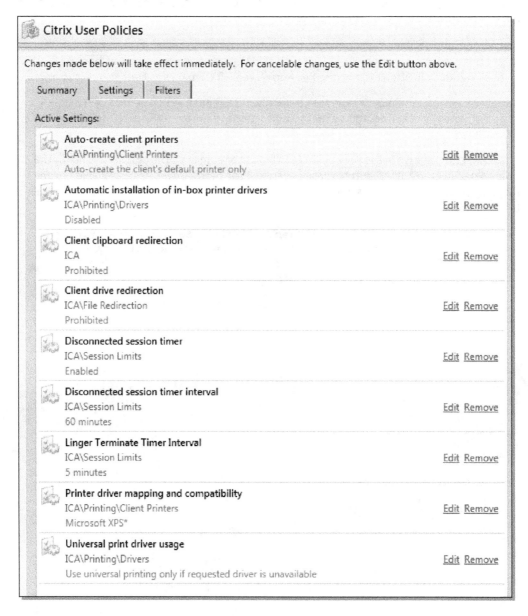

The final element of printing that we will cover here is the replication of print drivers. We have seen from the Group Policy settings that it is possible to implement a policy to prevent the user session from loading print drivers. In such a case, we may want to have some print drivers preloaded on our XenApp servers. This would be for printers that perhaps do not operate well with the Citrix Universal print driver, and consequently, the native driver is preferred and has presumably been tested. As an administrator, we can add the driver manually, but if we have several servers in the farm, it would be impractical to load on all servers. In such a case, we would load the print driver on one XenApp server and use PowerShell to set up replication of the driver to all existing and new XenApp servers as they are added to the farm.

```
Add-PSSnapin Citrix.XenApp.Commands
```

```
Add-XAAutoReplicatedPrintDriver -DriverName "Brother 166C" -SeverName XA1
```

With the previous command, we replicate the `Brother` printer driver from the XenApp server `XA1` to all other servers in the farm. As new servers are added, they too will receive the driver replicated from `XA1`.

> The printer driver is stored on the XenApp server, and the record to replicate it is stored in the IMA database. Drivers are never stored in the database.

Enabling IMA encryption

Each XenApp server within a zone needs to communicate to the **Zone Data Collector** (**ZDC**), if we have multiple zones, usually because of geographically separate data centers, then the ZDCs of each zone talk to each other. This communication uses the **Independent Management Architecture** (**IMA**) protocol, on TCP port 2512. If required, perhaps because you have multiple zones and the ZDCs talk over the WAN, your IMA communication within the farm can be encrypted. The tool to configure encryption is run from the command line, `ctxkeytool.exe`.

> Zone Data Collectors can only be elected from XenApp Servers that hold the Session Controller role. The data they store makes up dynamic farm information such as each server's load.

Firstly, we copy the `[XenApp-install-DVD]:\support\ctxkeytool.exe` file and the `[XenApp-install-DVD]:\support\resource` folder to a target directory on each XenApp server. The target directory could be something like `C:\Citrix`, as we use here. The directory, once created and populated, would look similar this this:

```
c:\Citrix\ctxkeytool.exe
```

```
c:\Citrix\resource
```

Once the first server into the farm is installed and rebooted, configure IMA encryption. With the following commands we generate a brand new key on the first XenApp server in the farm, we happen to call the key, NewFarmKey but the name can be anything appropriate to your environment. Replace <NewFarmKey> with the name you want to use for your key:

```
c:\citrix\ctxkeytool.exe generate <NewFarmkey>
c:\citrix\ctxkeytool.exe load <NewFarmkey>
c:\citrix\ctxkeytool.exe newkey
c:\citrix\ctxkeytool.exe query
```

With this in place, we now copy c:\citrix\NewFarmKey to each XenApp server and complete the configuration of each new XenApp server but we *don't* reboot. Before we reboot, we must load the key. So for each XenApp Server after they have joined the farm but *before* the reboot, we run the following command:

```
c:\citrix\ctxkeytool.exe load NewFarmkey
```

The IMA traffic using TCP port 2512 will now be encrypted between all XenApp servers within the farm.

Load management

If we have more than one XenApp server, and most installations would include multiple servers, we need to ensure that the user load is distributed across the farm evenly. Even within very small farms, being able to distribute the workload in your farm across more than one server makes great sense. Within Citrix XenApp 6.5, we assign load evaluators to servers using Group Policies. There are two load evaluators provided as standard: default and advanced. The default load evaluator looks at the number of users connected to the server, while advanced looks at CPU, memory, and page swaps. Both load evaluators include a login load throttle rule to prevent too many simultaneous logins to a server.

We cannot edit the system-supplied load evaluators, but we can copy them or create new load evaluators from scratch and include our own load evaluator rules. These rules range from IP Address to schedules, as well as more traditional load rules such as disk I/O.

It is the default load evaluator that is assigned to all servers if we have not implemented any changes. This will report to full load of 10,000 if 100 users are connected to the server. So, for each user connecting, a load increases by a metric of 100.

We can view the server's load by using the following command with PowerShell:

```
Get-XAServerLoad
```

Or, by using traditional command-line tools:

```
query farm /load
```

The output of the PowerShell command is shown in the following screenshot, and it indicates that a single user is connected when using the default load evaluator:

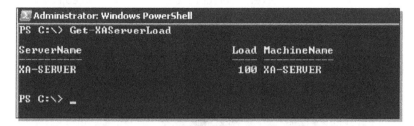

As a new connection is made, ZDC will have the session established on the least loaded server that hosts the requested resource. If the user has an existing session on a server, irrespective of that server's load, it will host the new connection so long as the server hosts the resource that the user requests.

While a user login is in process and Load Throttling is enabled as a metric, the reported server load is increased substantially during the login process. The load reported will reduce once the login process has completed. We can see this in action by viewing the output of the query farm /load command, while a user login is in progress. The following screenshot depicts the output of the command while a session is being established on the server (note the Load Throttling Load):

```
PS C:\> query farm /load
Server Name          Server Load   Load Throttling Load   Logon Mode
                     ───────────   ──────────────────     ──────────
XA-SERVER            200           5000                   AllowLogons
PS C:\> _
```

Load evaluators are assigned to servers via a computer Group Policy, and new load evaluators can be created using the **Load Evaluators** node in AppCenter. Computer policies are refreshed at the normal 90-minute interval or on a server restart. If we choose to use PowerShell to assign the load evaluator, we could use the following commands to set the advanced load evaluator in the unfiltered computer policy:

```
Add-PSSnapin Citrix.Common.GroupPolicy

Set-ItemProperty LocalFarmGPO:\Computer\Unfiltered\Settings\
ServerSettings\LoadEvaluator -Name Value -Value Advanced
```

The advanced load evaluator looks at the actual load on the server, reads the CPU, memory, and page swaps to calculate the load. We can see the difference in the reported server load with the same single user connected to my server; a server that is not well resourced,(1.2 GB RAM and 2 GHz processor), and more realistically reports being over 50 percent loaded at 5797, as shown in the following screenshot:

Consider using your own custom load evaluators that look at more obscure metrics to manage levels of security:

♦ **IP address**: With this metric we can make some servers unavailable to users who are not located on, for example, the corporate network. This way we could have some servers that are available to users accessing from outside of the corporate network and others servers with a higher classification that are accessible only from the corporate IP address range.

♦ **Schedule**: Again, enabling a schedule can improve security for some servers, where they will no longer accept new connections past certain times. These servers may well be available from 9 a.m. to 5 p.m., but outside of these hours the server will not accept any new connection. Perhaps then, users who try to access out of hours will be directed to servers that are permitted to service these requests.

These two rules would normally be combined with other metrics so that the actual load can also be in conjunction with the IP address and schedule.

Controlling access to servers

From the output that we saw from query farm earlier, we can see that there is a Login Mode for our XenApp servers. The default is **AllowLogons**. The following are the reasons why we may not want users to log on to XenApp Server:

♦ **Planned downtime**: It may be that we need to have a maintenance window for a server to apply hardware fixes, patches, and so on. For this reason then, ahead of the window we may disallow new logins to the server.

♦ **Dedicated data collector**: In larger farms it may be desirable to have XenApp Servers that act as the ZDC but do not host sessions. In this case, we can disallow logins to the server permanently.

To disallow logons to a server, use AppCenter. Right-click on the server and select **Other Tasks | Logon Control**. This is illustrated in the following screenshot:

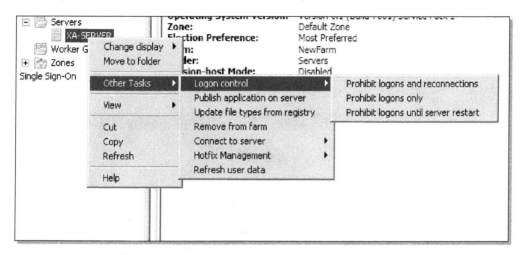

Alternatively, this can be set using PowerShell with the `Citrix.XenApp.Commands` snap-in loaded:

```
Set-XAServerLogOnMode -ServerName XA-Server -LogOnMode AllowLogons
```

The options available for the `-LogonMode` are as follows:

+ `AllowLogons`
+ `ProhibitNewLogonsUntilRestart`
+ `ProhibitNewLogons`
+ `ProhibitLogons`

The difference between a new logon and logon is if you have an existing connection to the server, you can make connections to new applications and resources on the server if `ProhibitNewLogons` is set. Whereas, if `ProhibitLogons` is set, even if you have an existing connection to the server, any connection to a new application or resource will be made to a different server.

Restricting the domains that can log on to the Web Interface

We can make life easier for our users by implementing restrictions. It may appear counterintuitive; however, a domain restriction does help our users. By default, users will need to add in their username, password, and domain to authenticate to the Active Directory. By restricting logins to a single domain, users only have to enter their username and password. If we restrict to more than one domain, users will need to select the domain from a drop-down list.

Using the Web Interface administration console from the Web Interface server, **Start | All Programs | Citrix | Management Consoles | Citrix Web Interface Management,** we can navigate to a Web Site, and using the right-click context menu we can select **Authentication Methods** and **Properties** of the `Explicit` method. From the properties page, we click on **Domain Restrictions,** which is found within the **General** section. It becomes a simple task to add in the domain. Although this reads as a restriction, I always read this as "user enablement"– we are making life easier by implementing this setting. The following screenshot illustrates the restriction to the `example` domain:

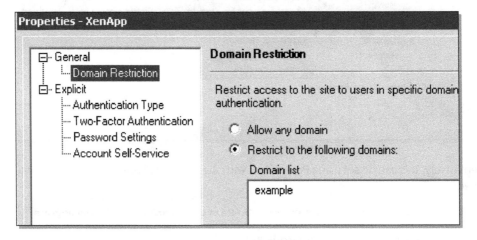

Changes made to the Web Interface site configuration are written to the `c:\inetpub\ wwwroot\Citrix\<nameofsite>\conf\webinterface.conf` file. Changes may be made directly to the file if preferred. The settings we have implemented here are listed as follows:

```
RestrictDomains=On

DomainSelection=example
```

Customizing the Web Interface

When users connect to the Web Interface server, they are presented with a very standard Citrix page. Even if you do not want to get involved with the images, you should at least change the text that is known as the **horizon tag line**. We can see this in the following screenshot:

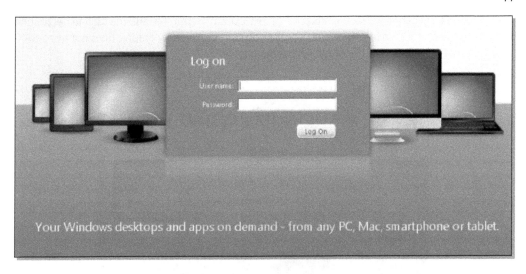

It is very easy to edit the bottom line of text that reads **Your Windows desktops and apps....** To change the text to something a little more representative of your organization, navigate to the file system of the Web Interface server and edit the `C:\Program Files (x86)\Citrix\ Web Interface\5.4.0\languages\accessplatform_strings.properties` file.

This may seem complex, but it is just a text file and can be opened in Notepad.

Locate the line that reads:

`HorizonTagline=Your Windows desktops and apps on demand - from any PC, Mac, smartphone or tablet.`

Change it to appear like the following line:

`HorizonTagline=For helpdesk support call extension 34289.`

Once this is in place, we can check the display of the Web Interface Web Site. If we want to replace the standard XenApp graphic (as I have in the image), add your own logo into the `c:\ interpub\wwwroot\Citrix\XenApp \media` directory, and make sure that your image is named `CitrixXenApp.png` and back up the original image if you so wish.

The following screenshot shows the replaced `CitrixXenApp.png` file and the tagline decorating the logon page of the Web Interface Web Site. As you can see, the new graphic does not need to have the same dimensions as the original XenApp logo:

Providing secure remote access to XenApp

The Web Interface, by default, will return the IP address of the XenApp Server to the client. This is fine and suitable if the clients are on the corporate network and have a route to private IP addresses assigned to the XenApp Server.

It is possible to use **Network Address Translation** (**NAT**) and map public addresses to each XenApp Server, but it is both impractical and undesirable. It is most usual to "proxy ICA" connections using the Citrix Access Gateway, or more recently it has been called: **NetScaler Access Gateway**.

To make use of ICA proxy connections, you will need to purchase a platform license for the Access Gateway; this can be used with a physical or virtual Access Gateway appliance. Detailed configuration of the Access Gateway is covered in *Citrix Access Gateway VPX 5.04 Essentials*, *Packt Publishing*.

In this starter, we will view the configuration required for the Web Interface to use the Access Gateway. Using the Citrix Web Interface Management console we can use the right-click context menu and select **Secure Access**. From the submenu presented, we can see that the defaults provide for clients that have direct access to the XenApp servers. Selecting the drop-down menu, we can change **Direct** to **Gateway direct**. We are then prompted to put in the fully qualified domain name of the Access Gateway, this must match the PKI certificate issued to the Access Gateway. HTTPS has to be used on the Access Gateway. There is also a selection to use Session Reliability (TCP Port 2598) connections and multiple **Secure Ticket Authorities** (**STA**), as shown in the following screenshot:

Specify Gateway Settings

Specify gateway server details for any user devices that access this site through the Access Gateway or Secure Gateway. <u>More...</u>

Address (FQDN): cag.example.local

Port: 443

☑ Enable session reliability

☐ Request tickets from two STAs, where available

 The STA issues the access token for client connections. The access token is built into the ICA files supplied to the client specifying the server to make a connection to. Each access token has a default time to live (TTL) of 200 seconds.

With this complete, and the Access Gateway configured, clients connect using HTTPS to the Access Gateway logon point, and the Access Gateway then acts as a proxy server and provides connection to the XenApp Servers on the private network using ICA on TCP port 1494 or ICA tunneled through TCP Port 2598 for HDX Session Reliability.

If we take a look at the following extract from the screenshot of a client connecting to an Access Gateway, we can see In the URL of the browser that the client first makes the connection to the Access gateway, and then is redirected into the private network and the Web Interface server:

https://ag.example.com/https/wi.example.com/Citrix/cag/auth/login.aspx

Citrix **XenApp**

Monitoring XenApp

Depending on the licenses that you have for XenApp, you may have access to monitoring using EdgeSight from Citrix. Basic monitoring is included with Enterprise and is more detailed with Platinum.

Using Computer Policies with Enterprise and above we can reactively monitor XenApp Servers with Health Monitoring and Recovery. With the policy enabled, certain critical services can be monitored, alerts raised, or services restarted to resolve issues.

However, even without the more premium editions of XenApp, we can monitor elements of the XenApp server performance using the reliable workhorse, **Performance Monitor**. Performance Monitor counters are specific to XenApp, which are installed with each XenApp Server, and we can query real-time information as to data collector elections, ICA latency, ICA bandwidth in use, and so on.

As the Performance Monitor tool in Windows has been around since the days of NT4, I think it is often overlooked as a tool to use today. However, it is as powerful as it has ever been, and many more advanced management tools rely on the counters from Performance Monitor. In the following screenshot, we see and extract some of the counters available to specifically monitor XenApp:

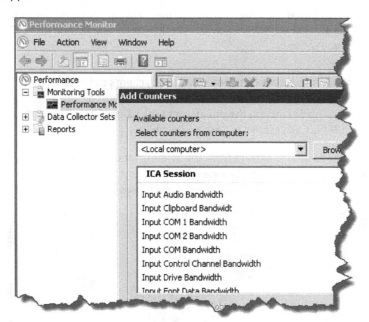

People and places you should get to know

Of course, one of the most valuable resources to the XenApp administrator is the XenApp community itself with their fora, wikis, and videos. Citrix plays a big part in this itself.

Official sites

+ You can visit the official website of Citrix at `http://www.citrix.com`.

+ You can also refer to Citrix eDocs at `http://support.citrix.com/proddocs/topic/xenapp/ps-library-wrapper.html`. This web portal is very useful– I know, we should always "read the manual", but in this case it is true.

+ CitrixTV contains videos from Citrix, both marketing and technical, relating to their product range and can be found at `http://www.citrix.com/tv/`.

Articles and tutorials

+ Personally, I maintain a list of Citrix tutorials, as well as other technologies and these videos and blogs can be found on my WordPress site at `http://wp.theurbanpenguin.com`.

+ *Brian Madden* is a VDI expert who blogs relentlessly on Citrix and other technologies at `http://www.brianmadden.com`, and he has to be on your must visit sites.

Blogs

+ You can refer to the blog of *Andrew Morgan* at `http://andrewmorgan.ie`. Andrew is an independent developer of ThinKiosk, a thin client computing solution, who knows huge amounts about Citrix and related remote access technologies.

+ *Ingmar Verheij* is one of the most influential people in the XenApp community. His blog entries are well respected and shared at `http://www.ingmarverheij.com/`.

+ *Trond Eirik Haavarstein* maintains the XenApp blog. A Citrix professional for many years, his site is current and up-to-date at `http://www.xenappblog.com`.

Twitter

+ Follow Andrew Mallett on `http://twitter.com/#!/theurbapenguin`.

+ Follow Citrix XenApp Team at `http://twitter.com/#!/xenappjunkie`.

+ For more Citrix and IT goodies information, follow Packt Publishing at `http://twitter.com/#!/packtpub`.

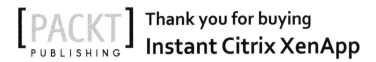

Thank you for buying
Instant Citrix XenApp

About Packt Publishing

Packt, pronounced 'packed', published its first book "*Mastering phpMyAdmin for Effective MySQL Management*" in April 2004 and subsequently continued to specialize in publishing highly focused books on specific technologies and solutions.

Our books and publications share the experiences of your fellow IT professionals in adapting and customizing today's systems, applications, and frameworks. Our solution based books give you the knowledge and power to customize the software and technologies you're using to get the job done. Packt books are more specific and less general than the IT books you have seen in the past. Our unique business model allows us to bring you more focused information, giving you more of what you need to know, and less of what you don't.

Packt is a modern, yet unique publishing company, which focuses on producing quality, cutting-edge books for communities of developers, administrators, and newbies alike. For more information, please visit our website: www.packtpub.com.

Writing for Packt

We welcome all inquiries from people who are interested in authoring. Book proposals should be sent to author@packtpub.com. If your book idea is still at an early stage and you would like to discuss it first before writing a formal book proposal, contact us; one of our commissioning editors will get in touch with you.

We're not just looking for published authors; if you have strong technical skills but no writing experience, our experienced editors can help you develop a writing career, or simply get some additional reward for your expertise.

Getting Started with Citrix XenApp 6

ISBN: 978-1-84968-128-5   Paperback: 444 pages

Design and implement Citrix farms based on XenApp 6

1. Use Citrix management tools to publish applications and resources on client devices with this book and eBook

2. Deploy and optimize XenApp 6 on Citrix XenServer, VMware ESX, and Microsoft Hyper-V virtual machines and physical servers

3. Understand new features included in XenApp 6 and review Citrix farms terminology and concepts

Getting Started with Citrix XenApp 6.5

ISBN: 978-1-84968-666-2   Paperback: 478 pages

Design and implement Citrix farms based on XenApp 6.5

1. Use Citrix management tools to publish applications and resources on client devices with this book and eBook

2. Deploy and optimize XenApp 6.5 on Citrix XenServer, VMware ESX, and Microsoft Hyper-V virtual machines and physical servers

3. Understand new features included in XenApp 6.5 including a brand new chapter on advanced XenApp deployment covering topics such as unattended install of XenApp 6.5, using dynamic data center provisioning, and more

Please check **www.PacktPub.com** for information on our titles

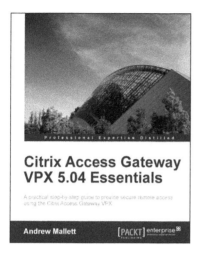

Citrix Access Gateway VPX 5.04 Essentials

ISBN: 978-1-84968-822-2   Paperback: 234 pages

A practical step-by-step guide to provide secure remote access using the Citrix Access Gateway VPX

1. A complete administration companion guiding you through the complexity of providing secure remote access using the Citrix Access Gateway 5 virtual appliance

2. Establish secure access using ICA-Proxy to your Citrix XenApp and XenDesktop hosted environments

3. Use SmartAccess technology to evaluate end users' devices before they connect to your protected network

Citrix Access Gateway VPX 5.04 Essentials

A practical step-by-step guide to provide secure remote access using the Citrix Access Gateway VPX

Andrew Mallett

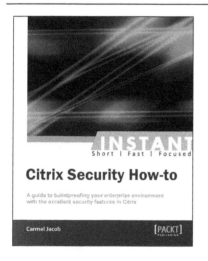

Instant Citrix Security How-to

ISBN: 978-1-84968-672-3   Paperback: 74 pages

A guide to bulletproofing your enterprise environment with the excellent security features in Citrix

1. earn something new in an Instant! A short, fast, focused guide delivering immediate results.

2. Simple and detailed security implementations for your existing or brand new Citrix deployments

3. Solutions to your network environment problems

Citrix Security How-to

A guide to bulletproofing your enterprise environment with the excellent security features in Citrix

Carmel Jacob

Please check **www.PacktPub.com** for information on our titles

www.ingramcontent.com/pod-product-compliance
Lightning Source LLC
Chambersburg PA
CBHW060444060326
40690CB00019B/4326